How To Survive An Apocalypse?

By Maxime STONE

PREFACE

Welcome to the ultimate guide to surviving a global disaster!

This guide is your go-to resource for everything you need to know to stay safe and thrive in the face of even the most extreme challenges.

From natural disasters to global pandemics, this guide covers it all. Inside, you will find expert advices.

But this guide isn't just about providing information - it's about motivating you to take action.

By following the tips and strategies outlined in these pages, you can become a true survivor, ready for anything life throws your way.

So whether you're a seasoned survivalist or just getting started, this guide is the perfect tool to help you prepare for the worst and hope for the best.

Not intended to teach you how to make a fire with a flint, how to kill a wild animal with a desert spoon or how to build a palace with a scrap pallet.

To explain all this in a small guide would have made a book of several kilos.

A video is much better to teach you some of the techniques that you can easily find on the net.

Think of downloading them on your disk or a USB key because it would be hazardous that the internet will be available at that time.

Table of content :

PREFACE 2

CHAPTER I: What do we mean by apocalypse?...................5

CHAPTER II: Understanding the Threats 8

CHAPTER III: Assessing Your Resources 12

CHAPTER IV: Creating a Survival Plan 15

CHAPTER V: Preparing for the Worst 19

CHAPTER VI: Building a Shelter..22

CHAPTER VII: Finding and Purifying Water 25

CHAPTER VIII: Finding Food 29

CHAPTER IX: Medical Care...32

CHAPTER X: Self-Defence 35

CHAPTER XI: Psychological Preparation 38

CHAPTER XII: Surviving in the City 40

CHAPTER XIII: Surviving in the Wilderness 43

CHAPTER XIV: Communication and Networking.................46

CHAPTER XV: Bartering and Trade......................................49

CHAPTER XVI: Rebuilding After an Apocalypse.................52

CHAPTER XVII: Staying Safe in the Long-Term 55

CHAPTER XVIII: Living Off the Grid 58

CHAPTER XIX: Balancing Individualism and Community ...61

CHAPTER XX: What conclusion can we draw?...................64

CHAPTER XXI: In the past..66

APPENDIX...78

CHAPTER I: What do we mean by apocalypse?

The word "apocalypse" comes from the Greek word "apokálypsis," which means "uncovering" or "revealing." The root word "kályptein" means "to cover" or "to conceal," while the prefix "apo-" means "away" or "off."

In religious contexts, "apocalypse" refers to the end of the world or a period of great turmoil and destruction, often associated with divine judgment. The term is often used in reference to the biblical book of Revelation, which describes a series of apocalyptic events leading up to the end of the world.

Outside of religious contexts, "apocalypse" can refer to any event or situation that involves widespread destruction, chaos, or upheaval.

An apocalypse is a catastrophic event that can wreak havoc, cause death and devastate societies. Natural disasters such as earthquakes, hurricanes and tsunamis, as well as human-made events like pandemics, nuclear warfare and cyberattacks can all lead to an apocalypse.

In this guide, we will explore the many different possibilities of an apocalypse and provide helpful advice on how to survive it.

It is essential to know that any time or place could fall victim to an apocalypse. While predicting when or where one may occur is impossible, we can arm ourselves with knowledge and resources in order to be better prepared for survival.

This includes educating ourselves on potential threats and having the right skillsets available so that we are ready for anything.

Mentally preparing oneself is also key in surviving an apocalypse. Having the right state of mind means being adaptable, creative, resourceful and able to think fast under pressure - all indispensable qualities during a post-apocalyptic situation.

It is essential to remain resilient in the face of the stress, trauma and loneliness that are often inevitable in these times of crisis.

Tips:
- Start by learning as much as you can about the potential threats that can cause an apocalypse. This includes researching historical events and current trends in natural disasters, pandemics, and human-made disasters.

- Take inventory of your current resources and skills and identify areas where you need to improve. This includes having an emergency kit, stockpiling food and water, and learning first aid and self-defence skills.

- Stay informed and up-to-date on potential threats and emergency protocols in your area. This includes signing up for emergency alerts and knowing evacuation routes.

- Connect with others who are also preparing for an apocalypse. This includes joining survival groups or attending workshops and training sessions.
- Remember that survival is not just about physical preparedness but also mental and emotional preparedness. Take steps to strengthen your mental and emotional resilience, such as practicing mindfulness or developing coping strategies for stress and trauma.

CHAPTER II: Understanding the Threats

We will explore various types of disasters that could potentially lead to an apocalypse.

By understanding the risks associated with each type of disaster, we can create a comprehensive survival plan that maximizes our chances of survival.

Natural disasters such as hurricanes, tornadoes, earthquakes, and wildfires can quickly destroy entire communities and disrupt essential services like electricity and water supply.

To prepare for these types of disasters, we recommend the following:

- Stock up on essential items such as food, water, medication, and first aid supplies.

- Prepare an emergency evacuation plan and identify safe shelters.

- Familiarize yourself with local emergency alerts and evacuation routes.

- Practice emergency drills with family and friends to ensure everyone is prepared.

- Secure your home and property by installing hurricane shutters, reinforcing doors and windows, and clearing debris.

- Pandemics can spread rapidly, leading to widespread sickness and death.

- To ready ourselves for pandemics, we recommend the following:

- Stock up on necessary items such as food, water, medication, and first aid supplies.

- Practice good hygiene habits such as washing your hands frequently and avoiding close contact with sick individuals.

- Avoid crowded places and wear protective gear such as facemasks and gloves when necessary.

- Stay informed about the latest developments and guidelines from public health officials.

- Consider being vaccinated when a vaccine is available and safe.

The threat of nuclear warfare is very real, and the devastation it can cause is immense.

To be adequately prepared, we must understand the potential threats posed by such conflicts and take appropriate measures in advance.

To prepare for a nuclear war, we recommend the following:

- Identify safe shelters and stock them with essential supplies such as food, water, and medication.

- Establish communication policies between family members, friends, and neighbors.

- Learn about radiation and its effects, and how to protect yourself from it.

- Monitor news and updates regarding nuclear threats.

- Consider purchasing radiation detection equipment and protective gear.

- Finally, while cyber-attacks, economic crises, and climate change may not cause immediate destruction, their long-lasting effects can be serious.

- To prepare for these types of disasters, we recommend the following:

- Educate yourself about the potential risks and threats associated with these types of disasters.

- Develop contingency plans for financial instability and consider investing in assets like gold and silver.

- Reduce your carbon footprint and take steps to reduce your impact on the environment.

- Backup important data and store it in a secure location.

- Consider investing in cybersecurity measures to protect yourself from cyber-attacks.

Understanding the various risks and threats associated with an apocalypse is essential to creating a successful survival plan.

By taking the necessary precautions and being prepared for the worst, individuals and communities can increase their chances of survival in the face of difficult times.

CHAPTER III: Assessing Your Resources

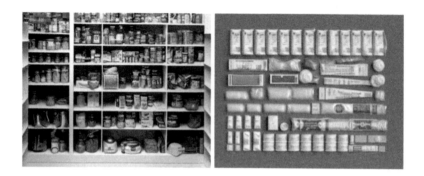

When assessing your resources in the event of an apocalypse, it is important to remember that these are only estimates.

Therefore, you must plan for the worst-case scenario and stock up accordingly.

You must take into account the longevity of supplies and ascertain how much can be replenished or replaced in a particular situation.

In anticipation of an apocalypse, having access to resources such as food, water, shelter and medical supplies is vital to survival.

We will outline ways to assess your resources and create a plan to be as prepared as possible in the event of a disaster.

Taking inventory of what you have is the first step in the process.

It is necessary to consider the condition of your shelter and any safeguards against potential threats that could occur during an apocalypse.

Once all current resources are considered, it is important to determine the amount needed per person to survive a potential apocalypse; this may involve researching the estimated amounts of food/water needed, as well as medical supplies and materials needed in the shelter.

For example, including information about recommended daily caloric intake and water consumption for survival can help you calculate the amount of food and water you need to stockpile.

To illustrate the importance of assessing resources and planning for the worst-case scenario, we provide six specific examples or scenarios:

1. A pandemic that affects the food supply chain, resulting in shortages and limited access to fresh produce and other perishable goods.

2. A natural disaster, such as a hurricane or earthquake, that disrupts water and electricity supply and makes it difficult to obtain necessary resources.

3. A nuclear war that contaminates water and soil, rendering it unsafe to consume and limiting food sources.

4. An economic crisis that causes hyperinflation, making it difficult to afford necessities.

5. Climate change that causes droughts or other extreme weather conditions that affect crop yields and the availability of water.

6. Cyber-attacks that disrupt essential services such as electricity, water supply, and communication networks.

Following these examples, it is clear that being prepared for an apocalypse is critical for survival.

Tips:
- Always plan for more than you think you will need. It is better to have extra supplies than to run out in a time of need.
- Keep your supplies organized and in a central location for easy access.

- Consider alternative sources of food and water, such as hunting, fishing, and rainwater collection.

- Consider purchasing a water filtration system or other means of purifying water in case your supply runs out. https://a.co/d/gKfxJDF

- Consider the needs of others in your group or community when assessing your resources.

CHAPTER IV: Creating a Survival Plan

Having a comprehensive survival plan is essential in any disaster situation.

Taking the time to assess your environment, create communication and evacuation plans, and practice with your family can mean the difference between life and death.

With careful preparation, you will be ready for anything that comes your way.

In times of disaster, speed is paramount. Developing an effective emergency strategy could be the factor between living or dying.

This chapter looks at how to generate a thorough safety plan so that everyone you love is prepared for any potential hazard that may arise.

First of all, it's crucial to evaluate the potential threats in your area. Think about what perils may appear and work out which ones are most likely to happen.

This could include natural disasters such as earthquakes, floods, or wildfires, or man-made disasters such as terrorist attacks or civil unrest.

When you have identified the greater threats, make a list of resources which will be needed to survive. This includes food, water, shelter, medical equipment, and other essential supplies.

Do not forget to consider the needs of pets or livestock in your care.

Another key component in any safety plan is having a go-bag on standby.

This bag should contain important documents, personal identification, cash, and other necessary items in case you need to evacuate quickly.

Secondary steps include creating a communication and evacuation plan.

This should include an agreed meeting point in case anyone becomes separated from the group due to lack of phone coverage, as well as an alert system to ensure everyone is safe and accounted for during such a time of distressful events.

Consider having alternative routes identified in case your main evacuation route is blocked.

Train regularly so that everyone applies the safety plan automatically.

This can involve running through possible scenarios and ensuring each person knows their role during such moments.

For example, practicing a fire drill or earthquake drill can help everyone understand what to do in the event of an emergency.

Specific examples or scenarios to illustrate the importance of practicing the safety plan with loved ones could include:

1. A family trapped in their home during a flood and needing to evacuate quickly

2. A group of friends hiking in the wilderness and encountering a dangerous animal

3. A couple stuck in their car during a blizzard and needing to keep warm while waiting for help

4. A family experiencing a house fire and needing to escape safely

5. A group of coworkers in an office building during an earthquake and needing to evacuate quickly and safely

6. A family needing to quickly evacuate their home due to a nearby wildfire.

Always check and update items within your go-bag and other supplies in case they need replacing or replenishing.

Having a sound preparatory strategy can prepare anyone when misfortune strikes.

By evaluating potential threats in your area, creating communication and evacuation plans, and practicing your safety plan with loved ones, you can be ready for anything that may come your way.

Tips:

- Consider purchasing a weather radio to stay informed during severe weather events.
  https://bestreviews.com/electronics/radios/best-weather-radios

- If you have children, make sure to involve them in the creation of your family's survival plan.

- Research the evacuation routes and safe zones in your area before an emergency happens.

CHAPTER V: Preparing for the Worst

When it comes to emergencies, being prepared can make all the difference.

In this chapter, we will discuss how to prepare for the worst-case scenario, including how to evaluate potential threats in your area, involve children in the family's survival plan, create communication and evacuation plans, and construct a bug-out bag.

Assessing Potential Threats:
Before creating an emergency plan, it is essential to evaluate the potential threats in your area. This is an important step in preparing for emergencies and should not be overlooked.

Involving Children in the Family's Survival Plan:
Parents should involve their children in the creation of the family's survival plan. Parents can explain to their children why it's important to prepare for emergencies and how they can help.

Children can be assigned age-appropriate tasks like packing their own go-bags or helping to create a family emergency kit.

Creating Communication and Evacuation Plans:
Communication plans should include how family members will stay in touch during an emergency, such as designated meeting places or emergency contact numbers.

Evacuation plans should include multiple routes to exit the area and safe zones to go to in case of emergency.

Constructing a Bug-Out Bag:
A bug-out bag is a compact collection that holds vital items required for survival in case of emergency. The pack should be easy to access and contain enough supplies that can last at least 72 hours.
Some essential items to include in your bug-out bag are:
- Water and water purification tablets
- Non-perishable foodstuff
- First aid kit
- Flashlight with additional batteries
- Multi tool
- Warm clothing and blankets
- Cash money and important documents

Practicing the Safety Plan with Loved Ones:
Practicing the safety plan can help identify any weaknesses or areas for improvement and ensure that everyone knows what to do in case of an emergency.

Fortifying Your Home If evacuation is not plausible, it is imperative to safeguard your home by creating a safe space for yourself and your family members.

Several ways you can strengthen your home include:
- Reinforcing doors and windows
- Boarding up windows
- Developing a safe room
- Possessing an alternative power source

Storing Food & Water For any disaster situation is crucial to have provisions of food & water that can endure over time.

Tips:
- Amassing non-perishable edibles such as canned goods, dehydrated fruits & veggies ,and cereals

- Keeping water in large airtight containers with added cleanliness tablets

- Rotating out any older foodstuffs or liquids regularly so they remain new

CHAPTER VI: Building a Shelter

When preparing for an apocalypse, finding or building a shelter is crucial to ensure survival.

Not only does a shelter provide physical protection from the elements, but it also allows for rest and storage of supplies.

However, before building a shelter, you have to evaluate potential threats in the area where the shelter will be constructed.

Building a shelter can be done using several methods, with functionality taking precedence over aesthetics.

This should take into account climate conditions, terrain characteristics, and potential dangers in the area, such as flooding.

One of the most efficient ways to construct a temporary shelter is to create a lean-to using either tarp or poncho.

This type of shelter requires securing one end to a sturdy branch or tree while tying down the other corners with rocks or heavy objects - making it both quick and effective in safeguarding against rain and wind.

Once the shelter is built, it will need to be monitored and maintained.

Regular inspections should be done from time to time to check for damage or wear and tear that requires immediate repair.

Improvements can also be made whenever necessary. Here are five examples of improvements that can be made to a shelter:

1. Adding insulation to keep the shelter warm in cold weather

2. Building a fire pit or stove to provide heat and cooking capabilities

3. Adding shelves or storage units to keep supplies organized

4. Installing a ventilation system to regulate air flow and prevent condensation

5. Creating a rainwater collection system for a sustainable water source

Tips:

- Prioritize function over aesthetics when building a shelter.

- Consider the climate, terrain, and potential threats in the area when building a shelter.

- Regularly inspect and maintain the shelter to ensure it remains safe and comfortable.

- Build the shelter on higher ground if the area is prone to flooding.

CHAPTER VII: Finding and Purifying Water

Access to clean water is essential for hydration, cooking, and sanitation, making it a top priority when preparing for an emergency.

However, in a post-apocalyptic world, finding clean water can be a challenge. To ensure your survival, you need to know how to find and purify water.

Evaluating Water Sources:
The first step is to know where to look for water. In any given area, water sources can include rivers, streams, lakes, and rainwater.

However, not all sources are safe to drink from. Before using any water source, you need to assess potential threats in the area, such as contamination from chemicals or sewage.

Specific information on how to evaluate potential threats in the area where you plan to find water is crucial in preparing for emergencies.

Identifying Safe Water Sources:
When looking for water, clear, flowing water that is free of debris is generally safe to drink.

However, some contaminants can be invisible, so it is best to purify any water you find.

In addition to assessing the water source itself, you also need to consider the container you use to collect the water. Make sure it is clean and sanitized to avoid contamination.

Purifying Water:
Even if you find a clean water source, it is vital to purify the water before drinking it.

Boiling is the most effective method for purifying water in a post-apocalyptic world. Bring the water to a rolling boil for at least one minute to kill any bacteria and viruses that may be present.

If you are unable to boil water, filtering and chemical treatments can be used.

Filtering:
Portable water filters are a convenient way to purify water in the field.

Look for a filter that is designed to remove bacteria, viruses, and protozoa.

It is important to note that filters have limited lifespans and need to be replaced regularly.

Chemical Treatments:
Chemical treatments, such as chlorine and iodine tablets, can also be used to purify water.

Follow the instructions on the package carefully, as overuse of these chemicals can be harmful.

Also, keep in mind that chemical treatments can leave a bad taste in the water, so it may be necessary to filter or mask the taste with other ingredients.

Tips:
- Always purify your water before drinking it, even if it looks clean.

- Keep a water filter and purification tablets in your bug-out bag.

- Boil water for at least one minute to ensure it is safe for drinking.

- Use a pre-filter to remove debris before using a water filter.

- If you do not have access to purification tablets or a filter, you can make a simple water filter using a cloth, sand, and gravel.

Natural filter

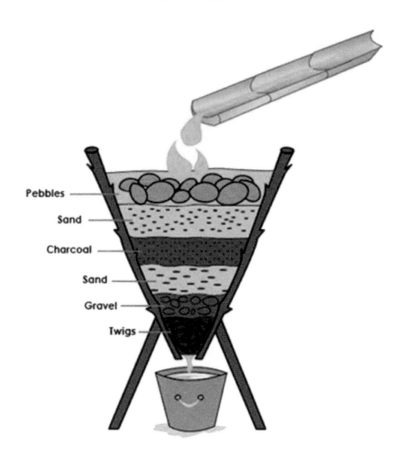

Pebbles
Sand
Charcoal
Sand
Gravel
Twigs

CHAPTER VIII: Finding Food

With the collapse of modern agriculture and supply chains, people will need to rely on their own skills and knowledge to obtain food.

Think about applying sustainable methods of obtaining food, and do not deplete the population or the environment.

Hunting is one of the most effective ways to obtain protein in the wild.

A skilled hunter can take down a variety of game, including deer, elk, and wild boar.

Hunting requires patience, knowledge of animal behaviour, and skill with a weapon, such as a rifle or bow and arrow.

Hunters must also be cautious of potential dangers in the area such as predators and other human hunters.

Fishing is another reliable method of obtaining protein.

Freshwater and saltwater fish can be caught with a variety of methods, including fishing rods, nets, and traps. In addition to fish, other aquatic animals such as clams, mussels, and crayfish can also be harvested.

Before fishing, assess the risks associated with the area, such as potential contamination of the water source.

Before consuming any fish or aquatic animals, they should be properly cleaned and cooked to prevent the transmission of waterborne illnesses.

Foraging for wild plants is another way to obtain food.

There are many edible plants in the wild, including berries, nuts, and mushrooms.

To use the local resource safely, you need to know about it to avoid poisonous plants and fungi. Some edible plants can also be used for medicinal purposes.

Foragers must also be cautious of potential dangers in the area such as predators and poisonous animals.

Domesticated animals such as chickens, goats, and pigs can provide a steady source of protein and other resources such as eggs and milk.

However, raising livestock requires a significant investment of time and resources, and animals must be protected from predators and other dangers.

Assess the risks associated with raising livestock in the area, such as potential predators and the availability of resources such as feed and water. Livestock should also be properly cared for and monitored for signs of disease or illness.

Tips:

- Learn about local wildlife and their behaviour to increase your chances of successful hunting and fishing.

- Know how to clean and prepare the animals you catch for consumption.

- Have a variety of tools for hunting and fishing, including different types of bait, lures, and traps.

- Learn to identify edible plants and mushrooms in the wild, and avoid poisonous ones.

- Consider raising livestock for a reliable source of protein and other resources.

CHAPTER IX: Medical Care

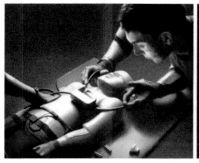 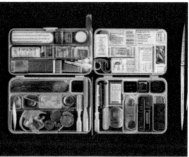

In a post-apocalyptic world, access to medical professionals and hospitals may not be possible. Therefore, it is essential for individuals to know how to provide basic medical care for themselves and others.

Creating a comprehensive first aid kit is the first step towards being prepared for a medical emergency.

Your kit should include basic supplies such as:
- Bandages
- Gauze
- Antiseptic
- Pain relievers
- Medical tape
- Thermometer
- Tweezers
- Scissors
- CPR mask
- 3 different Antibiotics

Keep the first aid kit <u>in an easily accessible location</u> and regularly check and restock it.

In addition to having a well-equipped first aid kit, individuals must also know how to use it effectively.

Basic medical skills such as cleaning and dressing wounds, treating burns, and caring for broken bones and sprains are essential.

Moreover, one should know how to handle common illnesses such as colds, flu, and infections.

However, some situations may require advanced medical techniques, such as administering CPR or using an epinephrine auto-injector to manage severe allergic reactions.

It is essential to know these procedures and have proper training and equipment.

Attempting advanced medical procedures without proper training and equipment can be dangerous and potentially fatal.

Therefore, individuals must be careful when performing any medical procedure beyond their level of expertise.

This includes being aware of the specific health risks in the area and knowing how to prevent and treat them where medical resources are scarce.

Tips:
- Make sure your first aid kit is easily accessible and regularly checked and restocked.

- Take a first aid course to learn more about providing basic medical care and advanced medical procedures.

- Consider including a medical reference book in your first aid kit, for quick reference in case of emergencies.

CHAPTER X: Self-Defence

Self-defence is a critical skill to possess during a survival situation, especially in an apocalypse.

In this chapter, we will discuss how to prepare yourself with the right tools and proper training to protect yourself and others during a crisis.

There are various self-defence tools available, including pepper spray, electric shock devices (tasers), knives, and firearms.

It is **imperative** to take heed that these tools should only be deployed after having received thorough training in their appropriate application.

Firearms, in particular, can be especially dangerous, attracting unwanted attention and potentially harming innocent bystanders.

Physical training is also valuable in self-defence. Martial arts styles such as Muay Thai, Krav-Maga, or Brazilian Jiu-Jitsu can offer valuable lessons in striking, grappling, and avoidance techniques that can be applied in confronting opponents.

Having strong physical abilities combined with good judgment ensures that one's self and loved ones are sufficiently protected from danger.

To further prepare yourself for a potential self-defence situation, it is recommended to review practical scenarios and case studies that can help you understand how to use these skills in real-world situations.

In addition to self-defence tools and physical training, situational awareness is essential to protect oneself and loved ones.

This means being aware of the people around you, their behaviour and body language, and being able to recognize potential threats before they occur.

Diplomacy is also a useful way to defuse situations without resorting to violence.

Ultimately, self-defence is a skill that requires proper preparation and training. By acquiring the appropriate education and equipment, any survivor can successfully navigate difficult situations and keep themselves and loved ones safe.

Tips:
- Choose a self-defence tool that you feel comfortable using and are well trained in handling.

- Practice self-defence techniques regularly to develop muscle memory and confidence.

- Be aware of your surroundings and potential threats.

- Invest in strong locks and reinforced doors for your home.

- Have a designated safe room where you can retreat in case of an attack.

CHAPTER XI: Psychological Preparation

In addition to practicing mindfulness and building a support system, it is crucial to establish a routine to maintain mental and emotional stability during an apocalypse.

Setting and achieving daily goals, such as finding food and water, fortifying shelter or exploring new territories, can help maintain a sense of purpose and direction.

Moreover, creating a sense of normalcy through routine can help reduce the impact of the apocalypse on mental health, such as maintaining a consistent sleep schedule, maintaining personal hygiene, and even participating in leisure activities like reading or playing games.

Furthermore, having a positive attitude can significantly impact mental and emotional wellbeing.

In spite of the circumstances, keep hope and remain optimistic because the morale acts on your physical.

Practicing gratitude and focusing on positive aspects of life can help maintain a positive attitude.

Finally, it is important to remember that seeking professional help is not a sign of weakness.

Surviving an apocalypse is a traumatic experience, and it is crucial to seek help when necessary to overcome any psychological challenges.

Tips:
- Practice mindfulness and stress-reducing techniques like meditation, yoga, or deep breathing exercises

- Build a support system with family, friends, or a community of fellow survivors

- Find ways to stay engaged in meaningful activities and maintain a sense of purpose and hope.

CHAPTER XII: Surviving in the City

Cities are inherently risky places to navigate during an apocalypse, and be prepared for any potential threats that may arise. Here are some tips to help you stay safe while exploring urban areas:

Plan Ahead:
Before you venture into any city, it is essential to have a map of the area and a clear plan in mind.

This will help you avoid dangerous areas and minimize the risk of drawing attention to yourself.

Shelter:
Abandoned buildings or businesses can provide temporary shelter, but always check beforehand to make sure they are free of potential danger or threat.

Consider parks or green spaces as an option as they may be more secluded than other areas within the city limits.

Supplies:
Dumpster diving can be risky in an urban environment, so approach this task with caution and strategy when searching for food, water, and other necessities such as clothing or medical supplies.

Visiting local stores or markets can also be beneficial if they are available nearby, but be aware of the risks of leaving your shelter.

Awareness:
No matter where you go in an urban landscape, remain aware of your surroundings at all times.

Avoid potentially hostile groups of people and stay away from dangerous areas to ensure a safe trip in cities, large or small.

By following these tips, you can increase your chances of survival while navigating through the city during an apocalypse.

Remember to stay alert, plan ahead, and be cautious in all situations!

Tips:
- Always have a map or plan of the area and stick to well-lit and populated areas.

- Avoid drawing attention to yourself and be aware of potential threats around you.

- Research and inspect any shelter options before using them.

- Look for parks or green spaces as safer alternatives for temporary shelter.

- Approach dumpster diving for supplies with caution and strategy.

- Consider visiting local stores or markets for necessities, but always prioritize safety when leaving your shelter.

- Stay aware of your surroundings at all times and trust your instincts.

- Carry a personal safety alarm or whistle.

- Avoid wearing flashy or expensive clothing and accessories.

- Travel with a group or a trusted companion whenever possible.

CHAPTER XIII: Surviving in the Wilderness

Navigating the wilderness during an apocalypse requires a combination of essential skills and preparedness. To ensure your safety and survival, it is essential to have a map, compass, and some basic knowledge of how to navigate.

Navigation:
Learn how to read a map and use a compass.

Utilize natural methods for finding direction, such as using the position of the sun and stars.

Always have a backup plan in case your primary navigation tools are lost or damaged.

Shelter:
Natural materials like branches, leaves, and rocks can be used to construct a shelter that is simple yet effective.

Look for natural features like caves or rock formations that can provide additional protection from the elements.

If you have a tent or tarp available, use it to provide added protection and insulation.

Food:
Fishing, hunting, and foraging for wild plants are all viable options for getting sustenance.

Learn how to identify edible plants and animals and what to avoid.

Always exercise caution when consuming any unknown plant or animal.

Storing and preserving food:
Learn how to properly store and preserve food to prevent spoilage.

Cooking over an open flame can help preserve food and provide warmth.

Tips:
- If you are lost in the wilderness, stay put and wait for rescue. Trying to find your way back can lead you further astray and make it harder for rescue teams to find you.

- Always bring a water purification method, such as iodine tablets or a filtration system, as drinking contaminated water can make you sick.

- Consider taking a wilderness survival course to learn more advanced skills and techniques for staying alive in the wilderness.

- Avoid consuming any unknown plant or animal to avoid potential poisoning or illness.

- Learn how to purify water from natural sources.

- Dress appropriately for the weather and terrain to avoid hypothermia, heat stroke, or other weather-related illnesses.

- Practice fire-making techniques and carry fire-starting tools like matches, lighters, or a fire starter kit.

- Be aware of potential dangers in the wilderness, such as wildlife, natural hazards, or hostile groups of people, and take necessary precautions to avoid or defend against them.

CHAPTER XIV: Communication and Networking

Access to news and updates can provide valuable information that could help you in your survival efforts.

To stay informed, it is good to have a way to receive news updates, whether it be through a radio or other communication device.

Having a plan for when things go wrong is also crucial, as well as an emergency kit with basic supplies such as food, water, and medical supplies.

Communication and networking are paramount for one's success during an apocalypse.

Obtaining the means of communication – from radios, satellite phones or even whistles – is essential for connecting with fellow survivors or signalling for help if necessary.

Additionally, establish relationships with other survivors as this provides safety in numbers while providing access to resources that may be scarce during such times.

Bartering and trading goods and services can create a sense of community and provide resources that would otherwise be unavailable.

To ensure one's survival during an apocalypse, stay informed of current events and any changes to the environment.

Establishing a network of individuals who can provide updates and news can be an effective way to do this.

Additionally, being aware of potential threats and developing plans of action should disaster strike without warning is essential for survival.

By taking the appropriate steps to ensure one's survival by establishing connections with others and staying informed on current events, individuals stand a greater chance at succeeding during chaotic situations.

Tips:
- Have multiple means of communication, such as a radio and a whistle

- Join or form a community of survivors to increase safety and access to resources

- Vet potential communities or groups before joining to ensure they align with your values and goals

- Use bartering and trade as a form of networking, but be fair and honest in your trades

- Develop skills that could be valuable to a community, such as medical training or carpentry.

- Be aware of potential threats and take measures to prevent or avoid them.

- Keep a low profile and avoid drawing attention to yourself when possible.

- Stay adaptable and open to new ideas and strategies for survival.

CHAPTER XV: Bartering and Trade

During an apocalypse, the value of money becomes less important as people prioritize more immediate needs such as food, shelter and safety.

To fill this gap, bartering and trading become essential means to acquire the necessary goods and services.

To barter effectively, know what items are in demand and have high value in the current market.

Basic items like food, water, medical supplies and ammunition will always be desired commodities that can be exchanged for other valuable resources.

Other items such as tools, clothing or fuel can also hold their own worth depending on the context of the scenario.

When engaging in bartering or trading, negotiate intelligently so you receive fair value for what you offer.

Being knowledgeable about the current market values of different products makes it easier to bargain with potential partners so you do not get taken advantage of easily.

Having good communication abilities and building trust between both sides are paramount when trying to make a successful deal.

A reputation for being fair and honest goes a long way when attempting future trades.

Building relationships and networks with other survivors can also be helpful in finding reliable trading partners.

Note that scavenging and looting should only be used if absolutely needed due to their hazardous nature.

When engaging in these activities, caution should always prevail.

Consider the ethics of taking resources from others who may be in need.

In summary, bartering and trading are essential skills to have during an apocalypse. By understanding what items are valuable and how to negotiate effectively, individuals can acquire the necessary goods and services to survive.

Building relationships and networks with other survivors can also be beneficial in finding reliable trading partners.

Tips:
- Keep a list of items you have available for bartering and trading.

- Understand the value and demand of the items you possess.

- Be willing to negotiate and compromise during bartering and trading.

- Don't undervalue or overvalue the items you're exchanging.

- Build relationships and trust with potential trading partners.

- Research and stay up-to-date on current market values for goods and services.

- Consider offering a variety of services or goods to broaden your trading options.

- Be cautious when scavenging or looting for goods.

- Avoid making enemies or getting a reputation for being unfair or dishonest.

- Be open to creative solutions and out-of-the-box thinking when it comes to bartering and trading.

CHAPTER XVI: Rebuilding After an Apocalypse

After surviving the initial chaos of an apocalypse, focus on rebuilding and forming a sustainable long-term survival strategy with others.

The first step is to assess the damage and define priorities.

This could include removing debris, restoring infrastructure, as well as setting up a reliable source of food and water.

Working together with others in the community can make these tasks more manageable and efficient.

Creating a secure living environment is also crucial for enduring survival.

Establish a defence strategy against potential adversaries such as raiders or infected persons, while also promoting a sense of safety and trust among community members.

Establishing a sustainable food and water supply is one of the most fundamental tasks in rebooting following an apocalypse.

This can be achieved through various means such as cultivating crops, fishing, or raising livestock.

Encouraging green practices, such as composting and using rainwater catchment systems, can also ensure that resources are not depleted quickly and remain available over time.

Generating energy sustainably is also essential for long-term survival.

Renewable energy sources like solar panels, wind turbines or hydroelectric generators can provide electricity for people's needs.

Be frugal and adopt conservation measures to reduce overall energy consumption in the community.

In addition, identify the skill sets needed within the population, creating communication systems between members, appointing leaders with authority over decision-making processes and preparing contingency plans in case of future disasters or attacks.

Regular reviews of these strategies can ensure that they remain relevant to changing times and continue to develop as the community grows.

Recognize that surviving an apocalypse can be a traumatic experience for individuals.

Encouraging open communication and providing psychological support to members of the community can promote healing and mental health.

Building strong relationships and a sense of community can provide a sense of purpose and hope for a brighter future.

Tips:
- Assess the damage and define priorities for rebuilding

- Create a secure living environment to safeguard against potential threats

- Establish a reliable source of food and water

- Use green practices to ensure resources are not depleted quickly

- Focus on renewable energy sources like solar panels, wind turbines, and hydroelectric generators

- Adopt conservation measures to reduce overall energy consumption in the community

- Identify skill sets needed within the population

- Create communication systems between members

- Appoint leaders with authority over decision-making processes

- Prepare contingency plans in case of future disasters or attacks.

- Consider establishing a community bank or bartering system to facilitate trade and sharing of resources

- Continually assess and adapt the long-term survival plan to address changing needs and circumstances.

CHAPTER XVII: Staying Safe in the Long-Term

Surviving an apocalypse is only the beginning of a long journey towards building a sustainable future in a new, dangerous world.

The aftermath of an apocalyptic event can leave lasting effects on the environment and the planet as a whole, making it crucial to remain vigilant and prepared for any future perils that may arise.

To stay safe in the long run, stay up-to-date with global and local news and information sources, and be aware of any impending threats or dangers.

This includes monitoring weather reports, geological activity, and other warning signs to anticipate potential natural disasters or environmental hazards.

Having strong allies and contacts within your network, such as friends or family members, can also provide critical support in times of crisis, so it is essential to maintain communication and connection with them.

In unfamiliar or dangerous situations, remaining vigilant and prepared is key to survival.

This can involve packing a survival kit, practicing situational awareness, and being prepared for any eventuality.

Be cautious when traveling and investigating unfamiliar areas, as they may be hazardous or contain hidden dangers.

To ensure long-term safety, be proactive and take steps to mitigate risks and potential dangers.

This can include taking measures to protect against disease, reducing environmental impacts, and establishing emergency protocols and contingency plans.

Tips:
- Keep a list of emergency contacts and important resources, such as hospitals, police stations, and community places.

- Develop a communication plan with your allies and contacts to ensure that you can stay in touch if regular communication channels are disrupted

- Stay up-to-date with global and local news sources to anticipate potential threats and dangers.

- Monitor weather reports and other warning signs for potential natural disasters or environmental hazards.

- Stay connected with allies and contacts within your network to provide critical support in times of crisis.

- Pack a survival kit and practice situational awareness when traveling or investigating unfamiliar areas.

- Be cautious and prepared for any eventuality in an attempt to survive.

- Establish emergency protocols and contingency plans to mitigate potential risks and dangers.

- Take measures to protect against disease and reduce environmental impacts.

- Regularly review and update your survival strategies and plans to remain relevant to changing times.

- Stay informed about the latest survival techniques and strategies.

- Develop valuable skills and knowledge that will increase your chances of survival in a dangerous world.

CHAPTER XVIII: Living Off the Grid

Living off the grid is not just about generating power and collecting water, but it is also about being self-reliant and independent from the mainstream society.

In a post-apocalyptic world, be able to provide for oneself and not rely on public utilities that may no longer exist.

To achieve self-sufficiency, one needs to start by assessing their needs and available resources.

This includes evaluating the climate, soil, and topography of the area, as well as identifying potential sources of food and water.

Generating power is a key aspect of living off the grid. Solar panels and wind turbines are excellent options for generating electricity, but they require an initial investment.

Ensure that the power generated is enough to meet one's needs.

Water is another essential resource for off-grid living.

Collecting rainwater and using a filtration system is a great way to ensure a reliable water supply, but having a backup water source is also crucial.

Know how to purify water and store it properly.

Growing a vegetable garden and raising livestock is an excellent way to be self-sufficient.

However, it requires knowledge and skills in gardening and farming.

Basic techniques such as soil preparation, planting, and harvesting are essential for success.

Knowing how to preserve food through canning, dehydrating, or smoking is also crucial for storing food for later use.

Storing food and water is essential for off-grid living.

Have a long-term storage plan, including properly storing food in a cool, dry place, and rotating it regularly.

Have a plan for waste disposal, composting, and recycling.

Finally, being self-sufficient also requires having basic medical knowledge and equipment and know how to treat common injuries and illnesses..

Tips:
- Assess your needs and available resources before deciding to live off the grid.

- Generate power using solar panels or wind turbines.

- Collect and filter rainwater, and have a backup water source.

- Learn basic gardening and farming techniques for growing vegetables and raising livestock.

- Store food and water properly for long-term use.

- Know how to preserve food through canning, dehydrating, or smoking.

- Have a plan for waste disposal, composting, and recycling.

- Learn basic medical knowledge and have access to essential medicines and equipment.

- Develop skills in self-defense and security.

- Consider joining a community of off-grid individuals for support and resources.

- Practice basic survival skills, such as building a fire and purifying water, in case of emergency situations.

CHAPTER XIX: Balancing Individualism and Community

The balance between individualism and community is essential for survival in an apocalyptic scenario.

While it is important to be self-sufficient and able to take care of oneself and one's immediate family, being part of a community can provide shared resources, safety in numbers, and support during difficult times.

Individualism:
The benefit of individualism is independence and self-reliance.

If you can take care of yourself and your family, you are less likely to be a burden on others, and you will be better equipped to survive if resources are scarce.

However, individualism can also have drawbacks.

Being completely self-sufficient may mean missing out on the benefits of being part of a community, such as shared knowledge, resources, and support.

Community:
Being part of a community has its advantages as well.

In a community, people can share resources and knowledge, work together to achieve common goals, and support each other during difficult times.

However, being part of a community can also have drawbacks.

If resources are scarce, there may be competition for those resources, which could lead to conflict within the community.

To find a balance between individualism and community, be self-sufficient enough to take care of yourself and your family, but also be open to collaboration and cooperation with others.

Tips:
- Start by building relationships with like-minded individuals who share your values and goals.

- Consider joining a community, such as a homesteading or survivalist group.

- Work on developing skills that can benefit both you and your community, such as gardening, hunting, or carpentry.

- Share your skills and knowledge with others, and be open to learning from them as well.

- Be aware of potential conflicts within your community, and work on resolving them before they become major issues.

- Create a system for sharing resources, such as tools or supplies, among community members.

- Consider developing a system for bartering goods and services within the community.

- Set up a neighbourhood watch or security system to keep the community safe from external threats.

- Plan for emergencies and disasters as a community, and develop an emergency preparedness plan.

- Maintain a balance between independence and interdependence, so that you can take care of yourself and your family, while also being open to working with others to achieve common goals.

- Consider joining a community or forming a small group of like-minded individuals to share resources and knowledge.

- Remember that in an apocalypse scenario, there is safety in numbers. By being part of a community, you can increase your chances of survival.

CHAPTER XX: What conclusion can we draw?

As we come to the end of this guide, we may feel overwhelmed by the task of preparing for an apocalypse.

It is easy to become consumed by thoughts of the worst-case scenario and lose hope.

However, remember that we are capable of adapting and surviving in the face of adversity.

In fact, history has shown that humans have a remarkable ability to overcome even the most challenging situations.

We have the power to work together, learn new skills, and innovate solutions.

So, let us approach the task of preparing for an apocalypse with a sense of hope and even humor.

While the situation may be serious, that does not mean we cannot find joy and laughter in the process.

Perhaps we can even see it as an opportunity to challenge ourselves, to learn new things, and to come together as a better community.

After all, we do not know what the future holds.

It may not be an apocalypse at all, but simply a series of unexpected challenges that require us to be resilient and adaptable.

So, let us embrace the unknown with a sense of curiosity and wonder, knowing that we have the power to survive and even thrive in the face of adversity.

As the saying goes, "prepare for the worst, hope for the best."

Let us do just that, with a smile on our faces and a spirit of resilience in our hearts.

CHAPTER XXI: In the past

As we have explored throughout this book, the possibility of an apocalypse is a very real and serious concern.

While we have discussed the potential risks and threats that could lead to an apocalyptic event, it is important to remember that humans have faced similar catastrophic events throughout history.

In this final chapter, we will take a look back at some of the most notable apocalyptic events in human history.

From natural disasters to man-made catastrophes, these events have left a lasting impact on our world and serve as a reminder of the fragility of human existence.

By examining these past events, we can gain a better understanding of the impact of an apocalypse and the importance of being prepared for such an eventuality.

So join us as we journey through history and explore some of the most significant apocalyptic events of all time.

The Bronze Age Collapse (12th century BCE):

A series of catastrophic events including invasions, droughts, and earthquakes that led to the collapse of several major civilizations in the eastern Mediterranean.

The Bronze Age Collapse was a period of significant upheaval and collapse that affected several major civilizations in the eastern Mediterranean during the 12th century BCE. This event was marked by a series of catastrophic events, including invasions, droughts, and earthquakes, that led to the decline and eventual collapse of civilizations such as the Hittites, Mycenaeans, and the city-states of the Levant.

One of the key factors contributing to the collapse was a series of invasions by the so-called "Sea Peoples," a group of seafaring raiders who attacked coastal cities and disrupted trade networks throughout the Mediterranean.

The invasions are believed to have been facilitated by a period of drought and climate change, which led to crop failures and famine in many regions. This, in turn, led to political instability and social unrest, with some regions resorting to raiding and warfare to acquire resources.

The collapse had significant impacts on the region, with many cities and settlements being abandoned or destroyed. Trade networks were disrupted, and cultural and technological knowledge was lost as a result of the collapse.

Some regions, such as Greece, experienced a period of decline and instability that lasted for several centuries.

The Bronze Age Collapse serves as a reminder of the fragility of even the most powerful civilizations, and the importance of resilience and adaptation in the face of catastrophic events. It also highlights the interconnectedness of human societies and the impacts that events in one region can have on others.

The Antonine Plague (165-180 CE):

The Antonine Plague, also known as the Plague of Galen, was an ancient pandemic that swept through the Roman Empire during the reign of Marcus Aurelius. It probably originated in the East and spread throughout the Empire through trade and military activities. The plague is named after Galen, a prominent physician of the time who described its symptoms and effects.

The Antonine Plague is estimated to have killed between five and ten million people, devastating the economy and military of the Roman Empire. The plague was particularly severe in densely populated urban areas and among soldiers stationed in close quarters.

This plague episode contributed to the decline of the Roman Empire by weakening the army and creating social and economic instability.

Despite its devastating impact, the Antonine Plague also had some positive effects. The need for medical treatment and research led to advances in the field of medicine, and the social and economic changes brought about by the pandemic paved the way for the rise of Christianity and other new religions.

Overall, the Antonine Plague is considered to be one of the deadliest pandemics in human history and a significant event in the decline of the Roman Empire.

The Fall of Rome (476 CE) is one of the most significant events in European history.

The Roman Empire had been the dominant power in Europe for centuries, and its collapse had far-reaching consequences. The period of decline and collapse of the Western Roman Empire began in the 3rd century CE and continued until the final collapse in 476 CE.

The decline was marked by a combination of political instability, economic decline, and military weakness. The empire had become too large to be effectively governed from a single center, and the political system was unable to keep up with the challenges it faced.

The economy was struggling, with inflation and taxation contributing to a decline in trade and a shortage of goods. Meanwhile, the military was overstretched and facing increasing pressure from barbarian invasions.

In 410 CE, the Visigoths sacked Rome, marking the first time the city had been captured in over 800 years. This event was a significant blow to the prestige of the empire and marked a turning point in its decline.

In 476 AD, the Germanic general Odoacer deposes the last Western Roman emperor, Romulus Augustus.

This event is often seen as the end of the Western Roman Empire.

The collapse of Rome had significant consequences for Europe and the wider world. The power vacuum left by the empire's collapse led to a period of political fragmentation and instability.

The economy suffered as trade declined, and the loss of the empire's extensive infrastructure meant that many people were left without basic services. The fall of Rome also had cultural consequences, with the loss of the Latin language and the decline of the classical tradition.

In conclusion, the fall of Rome was a pivotal moment in European history. It marked the end of an era of dominance by the Roman Empire and had far-reaching consequences for the political, economic, and cultural landscape of Europe.

The Black Death (1346-1353)

The Black Death, also known as the bubonic plague, was one of the deadliest pandemics in human history.

The death toll from this event is between 75 and 200 million people in Europe and Asia, with a mortality rate of up to 60% in some areas.

The disease was caused by the bacterium Yersinia pestis, which was transmitted through fleas that infested rats.

The pandemic began in Central Asia in the 1330s and gradually spread westward along trade routes. It arrived in Europe in 1347, when Genoese merchants brought it to the port of Messina in Sicily.

From there, it quickly spread throughout Italy and the rest of Europe.

The impact of the Black Death was devastating. It caused widespread panic and social unrest, as people struggled to understand what was happening and to cope with the scale of the disaster.

In some cases, villages and towns have been completely wiped out.

The economic impact of the pandemic was also severe. With so many people dying, there were labor shortages and a disruption in trade and commerce.

This led to inflation and economic instability, as well as social upheaval and political unrest.

Despite the horror of the Black Death, it did have some positive consequences. It led to improvements in public health, sanitation, and hygiene, as people began to understand the importance of cleanliness and disease prevention.

It also helped to break down feudalism and led to the rise of a more modern, urban society.

Overall, the Black Death was a catastrophic event that had a profound impact on the course of human history.

Its legacy is still felt today in the way we think about disease prevention and public health, as well as in the many cultural and artistic depictions of the pandemic that have survived over the centuries.

The Thirty Years' War (1618-1648) was one of the most devastating conflicts in European history.

It was fought primarily in what is now Germany and involved several major powers, including the Holy Roman Empire, France, Sweden, and Spain.

The war began as a religious conflict between Protestants and Catholics in the Holy Roman Empire, but it quickly escalated into a wider conflict involving political and territorial disputes.

The conflict caused widespread destruction, famine, and disease, leading to the deaths of millions of people.

The war's impact was felt across Europe, with many regions experiencing significant economic and social upheaval.

The war also marked a turning point in the history of warfare, with new tactics and technologies emerging that would shape military strategy for centuries to come.

The Thirty Years' War came to an end with the Peace of Westphalia in 1648, which established a new system of international relations and marked the beginning of the modern era.

However, the war's legacy continued to be felt for many years, as the region struggled to recover from the devastation caused by the conflict.

The Irish Potato Famine (1845-1849) was a devastating event that affected Ireland and its people.

The famine was caused by a failure of the potato crop, which was the main food source for the Irish population.

This was due to a disease that attacked the crop, known as the potato blight, as well as poor farming practices and government policies.

As a result of the famine, over a million people died and many others were forced to emigrate, mostly to the United States. The famine had a significant impact on Irish society and culture, and is still remembered today as a tragic event in the country's history.

During the famine, many people were forced to rely on soup kitchens and charitable organizations for their survival.

The British government, which ruled Ireland at the time, did little to help alleviate the crisis and even continued to export food from Ireland to other countries.

The famine also had a long-lasting impact on Irish agriculture and the economy.

Many small farmers were forced to give up their land and migrate, leading to a concentration of land ownership among wealthy landlords.

Overall, the Irish Potato Famine was a catastrophic event that had far-reaching consequences for Ireland and its people, both at the time and in the years that followed.

World War I (1914-1918):

World War I was a global conflict that began in Europe and involved multiple major powers, including Germany, Austria-Hungary, France, the United Kingdom, Russia, and the United States.

The war began in 1914 with the assassination of Archduke Franz Ferdinand of Austria, and quickly escalated into a full-scale conflict that lasted until 1918.

The war had a devastating impact on both soldiers and civilians. Millions of people died, and countless more were wounded or displaced.

The use of new technologies, such as poison gas and tanks, led to unprecedented levels of destruction and suffering.

The war also had significant social, economic, and political impacts. The war effort required massive amounts of resources, leading to rationing and shortages of essential goods.

Women took on new roles in the workforce and in society, leading to changes in gender roles and expectations.

The war also paved the way for the Russian Revolution and the rise of communism, as well as the breakup of the Ottoman Empire and the redrawing of national boundaries in Europe.

The aftermath of World War I had a profound impact on the world, setting the stage for future conflicts and shaping the course of history.

The Treaty of Versailles, which ended the war, imposed harsh penalties on Germany and helped create the conditions for the rise of Nazi Germany and the start of World War II.

The war also led to the establishment of the League of Nations, an early attempt at international cooperation and peacekeeping that ultimately proved ineffective.

Despite its devastating consequences, World War I marked a turning point in the history of the world, bringing an end to the old order and paving the way for a new era of political, social, and technological change.

The Spanish Flu (1918-1919) was a pandemic caused by the H1N.

This influenza virus infected an estimated 500 million people worldwide and killed an estimated 50 million.

The pandemic had significant social, economic, and political impacts. The virus was particularly deadly to young adults, which created a significant impact on the workforce and economic productivity.

The pandemic also led to social distancing measures, including quarantine, school closures, and the cancellation of public gatherings, which disrupted daily life and had economic consequences.

Furthermore, the pandemic occurred during the final stages of World War I, which had a significant impact on the war effort, as the virus affected soldiers and civilians.

The Spanish Flu pandemic ultimately ended due to a combination of factors, including the development of immunity among the surviving population, increased awareness of public health measures, and the evolution of the virus to a less virulent form.

The pandemic had a lasting impact on public health practices, leading to the development of modern infectious disease control measures, such as the widespread use of vaccines and antibiotics.

The Great Depression (1929-1939) was a period of severe economic downturn

This event affected many countries around the world. It began with the stock market crash of 1929 in the United States and quickly spread to other countries, leading to widespread poverty, unemployment, and political unrest.

The causes of the Great Depression are complex and include a combination of factors such as overproduction, unequal distribution of wealth, and speculation in the stock market.

The effects of the Depression were far-reaching, with many people losing their jobs, homes, and savings.

The unemployment rate in the United States reached a staggering 25%, and similar levels of unemployment were seen in other countries as well.

The Great Depression also had significant political consequences. In the United States, President Franklin D. Roosevelt's New Deal program aimed to provide relief and recovery efforts, as well as reform measures to prevent future economic crises.

The Depression also led to the rise of extremist political movements in many countries, such as fascism in Germany and Italy and communism in the Soviet Union.

Overall, the Great Depression had a profound impact on the world, shaping the course of history for decades to come.

World War II (1939-1945):

World War II was a global conflict that involved multiple major powers and resulted in the deaths of tens of millions of people, making it one of the deadliest conflicts in human history.

The war began with the invasion of Poland by Nazi Germany in 1939 and quickly spread across Europe and the world.

The war had a significant impact on the social, economic, and political landscape of the countries involved.

It marked the end of European dominance in the world and the rise of the United States and the Soviet Union as superpowers. It also saw the systematic extermination of six million Jews and other minorities in the Holocaust.

The war was fought on multiple fronts, including Europe, Africa, Asia, and the Pacific.

It involved the use of advanced weaponry and technology, including the atomic bomb.

The war ended with the unconditional surrender of Germany and Japan in 1945.

The aftermath of World War II had far-reaching consequences, including the establishment of the United Nations and the beginning of the Cold War between the United States and the Soviet Union.

The war also led to the formation of the European Union and the adoption of the Universal Declaration of Human Rights.

In addition to the loss of life and destruction of property, World War II also had a profound impact on culture, art, and literature.

Many works of art and literature were created in response to the war, including the classic novels "Catch-22" and "Slaughterhouse-Five."

Overall, World War II was a defining moment in world history, and its impact is still felt today.

It serves as a reminder of the devastating consequences of war and the importance of international cooperation and diplomacy.

APPENDIX

To go further into the experience and get more details on building and survival techniques in hostile environments, I recommend these 3 reference books:

"SAS Survival Handbook" by John "Lofty" Wiseman - This book is considered a reference for wilderness survival techniques. It covers topics such as navigation, shelter building, foraging for food and water, preparing for extreme weather conditions, and more.

"The Prepper's Blueprint: The Step-By-Step Guide To Help You Through Any Disaster" by Tess Pennington - This book offers a comprehensive guide to preparing for a wide variety of emergencies, from economic collapse to natural disasters to pandemics. It offers advice on planning, food and water storage, personal safety, shelter construction, and much more.

"Bushcraft 101: A Field Guide to the Art of Wilderness Survival" by Dave Canterbury - This book provides a practical introduction to wilderness survival techniques. It covers topics such as navigation, shelter building, foraging for food and water, tool making, and more.

Printed in Great Britain
by Amazon